25
B.

a LITTLE
HISTORY of
AUSTRALIA

D1393964

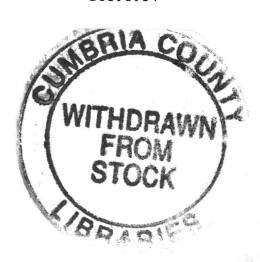

a LITTLE HISTORY of AUSTRALIA

MARK PEEL

Illustrations by Andrew Weldon

For Liz
Enjoy
Mark Peel
3/7/97

MELBOURNE UNIVERSITY PRESS

Melbourne University Press
PO Box 278, Carlton South, Victoria 3053, Australia

First published 1997

Designed and typeset by Lauren Statham in 9/14pt Galliard
Printed in Hong Kong

National Library of Australia Cataloguing-in-Publication entry

Peel, Mark 1959– .
   A little history of Australia.

   Bibliography.
   ISBN 0 522 84757 9.

   1. Australia—History. I. Title.

994

Acknowledgements

Some thought writing a history of Australia in 10 000 words was a crazy idea. After reading this book, some still might.

Many people helped me to clarify my thoughts, or simply endured the incessant, anxious chatter about what to do and how to do it: Val Campbell, Graeme Davison and Janet McCalman, who kindly read drafts; friends in the History Department at Monash University, especially Bain Attwood, Jane Drakard, Esther Faye, Peter Howard, Andrew Markus and John Rickard; Julie Tisdale, who helped me teach the course this story is drawn from; Sheryl Burgess, Nick Fischer, Piers Lumley, Stephen Powell, Geoff Robinson, Jeremy Sammut, Paul Sendziuk and Louise Walker, who shared a reading group and a lot of ideas; Louise Persse, John Stapleton, Philip Peel, Madeleine Pitcher and Cathy Emery; and the students in 'Imagining Australia's Tomorrow' in 1996 whose good humour and enterprise made the experiment work. I am also grateful for Michael Cathcart's skilled reading.

I want to thank Andrew Watson for trusting me with his idea, and Allison Jones for her enthusiastic assumption that it would actually work. I owe most to my editor, Susan Keogh: if this little history has anything to say, she has helped me to say it.

Illustrations

The following artworks are the basis for some of the text illustrations: James Cook's *Endeavour* beached for repairs after an engraving taken from the original drawing by Sidney Parkinson (p. 12); a convict haulage gang, inspired by a contemporary painting (p. 20); 'Return of Burke and Wills to Cooper Creek' by Nicholas Chevalier (p. 22); 'I have got it' by Eugène von Guérard (p. 28); 'The Pioneer' by Frederick McCubbin (p. 34); 'Down on his Luck' by Frederick McCubbin (p. 38); 'The Opening of the First Commonwealth Parliament' by Tom Roberts (p. 40); photograph of Private William Johnson being helped by Sergeant G. Ayre by Damien Parer (p. 64); 'Sunbaker', photograph by Max Dupain (p. 72).

Preface

NEW LANDS are discovered slowly. Glimpsed, but ignored for the day's catch or the real destination, they are remembered in stories and images. They are imagined for their prospects and their potential terrors, for what lies beyond their meeting with the sea and the half-seen stillness of their horizon. If others have come before you, who might they be? Are there wonders and monstrosities beyond imagining, or has everything which exists already been found?

Discovery and exploration are never blind. The land may be new or old, yet everyone who comes imagines it before they arrive. Tens of thousands of years ago, and then again during the seventeenth and eighteenth centuries, Australia was a new land. For its first discoverers, exploring the inlets and river mouths of the northern coast, for the Europeans who 'found' it again, first by chance and then by design, and for all those who came after, Australia might be a new home, or a place to serve out time. Or it might be a place to pass through, returning to another home richer than when you left.

'Australia' was made as the people of the past imagined that they shared a place and, more important, that they shared a future. Imagining a common destiny —as a 'people', a 'colony' or a 'nation'—was not the only story in Australia's past, nor did it dominate everyday life. It never included every Australian, because only some people could assume that their version of the future should be everyone's. Yet that future was never just theirs to make. 'Australia', as a country made by ancestors or a loose collection of colonies, emerged as people argued about what had been and what should be, and steered their course towards tomorrow. Australia's history is not just what happened, nor even how it did. It traces the paths not taken, and the futures which, for good reasons and bad, did not come to be.

European ships broke themselves upon
the reefs of the north-west.

I

IN THE seventeenth century, European ships stumbled and sometimes broke themselves upon the reefs of the north-west coast. Convinced there were rich lands south of the East Indies, others searched more purposefully. Combining the uncertain descriptions of Chinese, Arab and Greek geography, the Portuguese, Spanish and Dutch sought and found the southern land, and were disappointed. Dutch captain Willem Jansz reported of Cape York in 1606 that "there was no good to be done there", and the extensive voyages of Abel Tasman in the 1640s yielded little joy for his sponsors in the Dutch East India Company. English adventurer William Dampier confirmed such views on two voyages to 'New Holland' in 1688 and 1699. Arid and barren, it scarcely supported "the miserablest People in the world". The Europeans, interested in quick profits and compliant customers, were unimpressed.

Later, the British explorers who discovered Australia again had different aims for a new land. Their advance guard resembled floating scientific laboratories more than ships of war. Relative latecomers to the business of conquering, the British made heroes of botanists, not marauding *conquistadores*. As Captain James Cook found in his journey along the eastern coast in 1770, the continent certainly contained oddities enough to fascinate his men of science, and bounties sufficient to imagine a future of agriculture and civilising settlement.

Cook was fully aware that the land was inhabited. He was also more disposed to recognise the humanity of the people who already lived in New South Wales: "they may appear to some to be the most wretched people upon Earth, but in reality they are far more happier than we Europeans". These were clearly savages in British eyes, but that did not render them inhuman, or mean they had no right to expect protection from the law. Cook claimed sovereignty in the name of George III, but the short ceremony at Possession Island in 1770 did not resolve questions about who owned the land; it simply meant that no other European power could hope to establish itself there.

Neither Cook nor Arthur Phillip, the colony's first governor, would have agreed with the contention that British sovereignty inevitably meant that the Aboriginal occupiers lost all rights to the land. They could be legally dipossessed, but only if the land was virtually uninhabited or if they were shown to lack the possessive habits of civilised people. On the first point, Aboriginals were more numerous than the colonisers expected. On the second, First Fleet officers like Watkin Tench recognised that Aboriginal people did occupy and use the land. At this time, there was no final, authoritative decision on whether New South Wales was indeed *terra nullius* (legally unoccupied). No matter, for within a generation, a much simpler desire for land replaced such legal niceties with a violent assault upon 'the savages'.

Tench, Phillip and other officials always presumed that Europeans were civilised and Aboriginals were not. Yet there were moments of communication and even mutual respect in those first years which might have set the colony's race relations on a different course. The tragic momentum of misunderstanding, revenge and retaliation that turned Australia's frontiers into a killing zone for so much of the nineteenth century grew from choices and decisions; it was not inevitable.

During the twentieth century, with the work of conquering and clearing the land nearing completion, the need to portray Aboriginal society as disappointingly primitive or irredeemably savage slowly diminished. Some whites began to listen to the continent's original occupiers, and the discovery of Australia continued. Twentieth-century archaeologists and anthropologists painted an absorbing picture of a society and culture almost destroyed by European violence, diseases and ignorance. Their first descriptions of a splendid 'stone age' isolation, a society somehow frozen in time, were replaced halting appreciations of Aboriginal people as active discoverers and users of the land in their own right. They had been here at least forty thousand years and probably more. More than a million people may have been living in Australia in 1788.

Anthropologists, and others who cared to listen, heard Aboriginal stories of the beginning, the Dreaming. They began to comprehend how the landscape was sung and told into meaning and recognised by the signs of spirits passing and resting. Among a nonliterate people, life's origins and purposes were told in ceremonies, in art and in oral culture. The story of Australia's discovery could include new characters, people who actively shaped and changed the land and its plant and animal life. Aboriginal farming and hunting practices, especially the use of fire, had dramatic effects on the ecology of forests, plains and coasts. Different Aboriginal peoples created or appropriated tools, and traded with the peoples of New Guinea and Indonesia.

The story of Australia's frontier was also retold, with Aboriginals as actors rather than passive victims. There was resistance, although it was sporadic guerilla warfare rather than full-fledged defence. And how did contact look from the Aboriginal side of that frontier? It is difficult to imagine the shock that accompanied the arrival of the Europeans for a people who believed they were alone on the earth.

With Europeans came epidemics of smallpox and measles, which almost destroyed some communities, while sexual contact introduced venereal disease. Europeans also disrupted hunting territories and spoiled waterholes. Aboriginal reaction to this invasion was always complex. Some were curious, going out to meet the new arrivals, taking advantage of new foods like flour, hunting the ponderous cow and the artless sheep. Others kept away.

In general, Aboriginal people tried to incorporate Europeans within their own systems of exchange and hospitality. They tried to negotiate, to establish mutual respect for territory, and to minimise conflict. Most observers noted that Aboriginals expressed little desire to assimilate into European society. Instead, they expected Europeans either to move on, or to recognise the superiority of Aboriginal ways. But that prospect receded as the settlers kept coming and Aboriginals realised that these newcomers wanted to own the land, not share it. There was little hope of bargaining with them. They were here to stay, and so were their fences, their guns and their possessive ways.

The battle over land built slowly, because the colony's expansion was constrained by its main function as a prison. Whatever the other possibilities of a new territory—timber for British ships, the East Asian trade, or staring down the inquisitive French—Britain's need for a new overseas gaol justified creating an outpost half-way around the world. American revolutionaries had robbed Britain of its usual banishing place and, with full hulks moored on the Thames, Botany Bay— or, rather, the more promising inlet of Sydney Cove— became the replacement end of the earth.

So the first white settlers were male and female convicts, the soldiers to guard them, and the officers to plan and administer a penal colony. Between 1788 and the ending of transportation in the middle of the nineteenth century, around 160 000 convicts were sent to the colonies, about half to New South Wales. More than a quarter were Irish Catholics; many of the English convicts were from London. Most committed theft, in a society where extremes of wealth and poverty made the rich exceedingly anxious about even petty crime. Others participated in rural protests, or had the nerve to form trade unions.

Expelled, convicts lived in a prison which, once it could feed itself, offered them either vague salvation

Convicts dreamed of living unchained
and unleashed.

or certain retribution. Most survived as best they could. When assigned to private settlers, they saw themselves as temporary servants, not slaves. The future lay in the end of their sentence, a pardon or a 'ticket of leave' which allowed them to sell their labour. For those who rebelled, there were greater cruelties. For men, brutal flogging, or the 'secondary punishment' sites such as Norfolk Island; for women, harsh confinement in the Female Factory. Small wonder that some convicts dreamed of imaginary lands where people lived unchained and unlashed, and fled Sydney or Hobart to find them.

The boundaries between convicts and free settlers were sources of tension and anxiety. Within a few years of Sydney's founding, Phillip was asking for voluntary migrants from Britain, while ex-convict 'emancipists' were taking grants of land and labour. Native-born children added another complication. When relatively few were free, the benefits of freedom were great

Explorers followed rivers into the interior.

indeed; short-term trade in rum or more far-sighted experiments with raising sheep soon concentrated wealth and power in the hands of men like John Macarthur.

Sheep meant more land and more exploring. Farmers quickly followed those who, in 1813, found a way through the Blue Mountains west of Sydney. Though reluctant to permit uncontrolled expansion, the colonial government could do little to prevent illegal 'squatters' from simply grabbing the land. Meanwhile, explorers followed rivers into the interior, each hoping to join the ranks of intrepid English discoverers. Often disappointed, some paused long enough to retaliate with place names like Desolation Hill.

The colonies taking shape around the edges of the continent were not yet fixed on one future. By 1824 New South Wales had established new outposts in Van Diemen's Land and Moreton Bay. In these colonies, the emancipists tried to remove the stigma of their convict past. Other colonial ventures determined to be free of that stain from the beginning. In 1829 a new colony at Swan River in Western Australia sought private settlers, an experiment which lasted until 1846 when shortages of everything encouraged the few who remained to seek convicts instead. Edward Wakefield's 'systematic colonisation' fared better in South Australia, founded in 1836. Here, and in the Port Phillip settlement, the founders also promised more humane treatment for indigenous people. Unfortunately, that lasted only until land-hungry settlers found Aboriginals in their way.

By the 1840s many colonists believed their society to be in transition. Caroline Chisholm and other advocates of assisted free migration argued that in Australia Britons could "escape the continual struggle they endure". Australia should be a better place than Britain, not its replica. For those who knew they were born to rule, however, transition brought insecurity, especially in a world of former convicts and their children.

British views of the colonies were also changing. In 1819, London-appointed commissioner John Bigge recommended reinforcing the division between convict and free, and making transportation both more horrible (by sending recalcitrant convicts to Port Arthur and Moreton Bay) and a lot cheaper (by assigning more convicts to private masters who would have to feed and clothe them). Yet just twenty years later, the British Government's Molesworth Select Committee declared that the convict system had degraded free and convict alike and recommended an immediate end of transportation to New South Wales.

Many colonists knew they were "a rising generation", on a par with the people of any other British colony. Yet they feared that theirs might still be a degraded society. In the 1830s and 1840s, two arguments helped resolve that tension. First, convicts could reform, and they and their children would fill the country with an "industrious and virtuous agricultural population". Secondly, the colonies' lack of progress stemmed not from a dubious convict inheritance but the arbitrary rule of British authorities, as shown in their decision to resume transportation in 1848 without recognising that many colonists no longer regarded their society as Britain's gaol.

Protests aside, most free or freed settlers were preoccupied with making a new life in a new land, while wealthy squatters worked hard maintaining their advantages. Some also began imagining a specifically

Australian future, a British world, but one in which British virtues flourished at the expense of British vices. Yet optimism was always tinged with anxieties over the convict past, especially in a society about to be shaken by the rush for gold.

Gold fascinated settlers. Discoveries brought gold rushes, first in 1840s California, then in New South Wales and Victoria in the 1850s and Queensland a decade later. The last great rushes stirred Kalgoorlie in Western Australia and Canada's Yukon in the 1890s. In the Australian colonies, gold led to rapid immigration and transformed Victoria from part of New South Wales into a colony challenging its parent for supremacy. Gold also changed people's visions of the future.

For patriotic preacher John Dunmore Lang, gold was proof that Australia would reach "a height of prosperity and power which reduces the boasted growth of America to a size and height no longer astonishing". Lang even foresaw a United Provinces of Australia incorporating New Zealand and a Pacific Empire, its flag adorned with a kangaroo and seven stars.

Gold turned the world upside down, stripping cities and populating creeksides. As men poured into Victoria, the diggings increasingly resembled the kind of society respectable colonists had wanted to leave behind: uncivilised, unstable, footloose men in tents and shanties without the tempering influence of women and family.

Gold was arbitrary. It elevated people suddenly, disrupting the conviction that the wealthy were better people, not just better money-makers. Gold brought friction, as diggers assaulted Chinese miners on the fields. And the diggers were radical democrats, or so it appeared. The short battle at Ballarat's Eureka Stockade, where troops and police killed about thirty miners, mostly concerned exorbitant licence fees and administrative corruption. But powerful men like John Macarthur nervously predicted a "turbulent and immoral democracy". In the middle of the nineteenth

Gold turned the world upside down.

century, rulers feared too much democracy far more than too little.

While protesting miners, and protesting workers in the major cities, used a radical language, they wanted an orderly and stable world, not revolution. Democracy and more equal access to land promised them inclusion in colonial society. In response, the gentry founded public libraries and museums to maintain civilised values and to save the colonies from the "vile abominations" of "republican America".

The thirst for gold taught many colonists, radical, liberal and conservative alike, that materialism and economic competition were too dangerous to be left unchecked. Australia's best hope lay in securing a stable and prosperous British society which the corrupted old world could not provide and which other new worlds, like America, had not achieved.

During the last half of the nineteenth century, misgivings about the future belied the apparent confidence of colonial society. Each newly formed parliament spent public money securing economic expansion, only to be undone by speculative booms and busts. While South Australia's wealthy consolidated their money through prudent decisions and even more prudent marriages, riches in other colonies were as often spectacularly lost as gained. Colonial politicians did not let high-minded ideals get in the way of making profits.

Self-government and greater independence from Britain fuelled concerns about colonial security. Fears of Russian attack during the Crimean War in the 1850s led to a flurry of fort-building. In the 1880s the French occupied New Caledonia and the Germans New Guinea. Anxious colonial governments urged Britain to action. Queensland even annexed the southern part of New Guinea in 1883, athough this was overruled by a British government aware that the colony really wanted more 'natives' to work in its booming sugar industry.

Eager to remain thoroughly British, the gentry formed 'acclimatisation' societies to introduce European animals and plants. If the society balls and hunting parties proved tiresome, they could make occasional visits 'home' to see the real thing. But for most people, the 'coming Australian', though recognisably British, should improve the original model. Earnest displays of colonial success, like Melbourne's 1866 Inter-colonial Exhibition, insisted that the Australian colonies would match "European kingdoms in all that is worthy of rivalry". Yet at the same time, anxieties about an 'inverted' continent's manners and morals were matched by scientific speculations that Australia's inferior soil and hot climate would cause "an inevitable degeneration of the Anglo-Saxon stock".

The same science of 'stock' and 'breed' provided anxiety's antidote: as writer Rolf Boldrewood claimed, since "race is everything", the triumph of "the great Aryan stock" could not be hindered by mere location. In such a science, there were casualties. The status of the Irish was ambivalent, while the Chinese and the "Hindoos" were clearly subordinate. More profound still were the implications for Australia's Aboriginal people. Apparently doomed by what one writer called "natural laws", they deserved sympathy as a dying race. On the frontier, gradual extinction was too slow, and violent dispossession continued across Queensland, the Northern Territory and Western Australia.

By 1888, when New South Wales reached its centenary, anxieties about progress were stilled by the rapid growth of colonial cities, the development of compulsory education systems, and the number of imposing public edifices. Victoria and the other colonies were less than enthusiastic about Sydney's birthday, which included plans for a gigantic statue of 'Australasia', but few disagreed that Anniversary Day marked the birth of a British nation and "a civilisation of the highest type".

II

A LL THROUGH the 1890s, at the moment of Federation in 1901, and for a good decade afterwards, different people had different 'Australias' in their heads, different hopes and fears for a new country marooned so far from its 'Anglo-Saxon' beginnings. Artists and writers identified a distinctively Australian ethos in the common people and the commonplaces of 'the bush'. As the painters of the Heidelberg School captured Australia's squinting light, essayists and poets invented a story of self-reliant people whose fiercely democratic temper, according to their self-appointed spokesmen in the *Bulletin* magazine, set them against "the tyrant-ridden lands of Europe". The story was nostalgic even as it was being invented. Most of those producing it knew little of the bush, and those who did, like Henry Lawson, were usually careful to distinguish the people from the hardness of their place.

Self-reliant people

As the century neared its end, other writers explored Australia's destiny through fantasy. One popular genre told of lost civilisations in the desert; their ripping yarns of marvellous cities overwhelmed by volcanic eruptions hinted that even highly advanced societies were very fragile. Meanwhile, in Henrietta Dugdale's *A Few Hours in a Far-Off Age*, with its fully liberated twenty-third-century females, fantastic fiction expressed a rather different future for women.

For the feminists of the 1890s, it was self-evident that the highest development of Anglo-Saxon civilisation meant elevating Australia's women. Sydney feminist Louisa Lawson urged women to take up "the task of hastening humanity with surer and more certain steps towards the goal of justice, truth and mercy". Direct participation in politics was one means to that end; South Australia achieved women's suffrage in 1894, followed by Western Australia in 1899. The gains of a new womanhood were less clear for working women. Yet if the vote, easier divorces, more equal marriages and laws to curb 'men's vices' like drunkenness stepped on a few male toes, the assumption that a progressive civilisation needed a New

Woman held strong. Australian feminists made sure that the 'founding fathers' of federation would have to talk about female as well as male citizens.

Workers also talked of profound change. In the 'new unionism' of William Spence, ideals of workers' unity joined an assumption of basic class antagonism. For journalist William Lane, a 'paradise' for working men rested on the inevitable victory of socialism over capitalism. Events in the early 1890s certainly revealed deep social divisions. Employers used 'scab' labour to break a maritime strike. Shearing unions won some concessions in 1890, but were shattered by an employer counter-offensive in 1891. These confrontations pitted strikers against police and hastily mobilised 'special forces', and convinced many unionists of the need to secure their own political representation.

At the same time, Melbourne's land boom collapsed, and a severe drought exposed the fragility of the over-expanded pastoral economy. By 1893, banks were crashing as British investors pulled out of a rickety financial system. A timely gold rush insulated Western Australia, but in every other colony economic collapse revealed just how close to poverty's edge most small farmers and urban workers lived.

As people surveyed the ruins of their own hopes for the future, the proven vulnerabilities of a colonial economy fuelled anxieties about Australia's place in a threatening world. The great strikes also revealed that divisions were not based simply on intercolonial rivalries or the long-running political debate between advocates of tariff protection and believers in free trade. Australians' different loyalties promoted combat, not harmony. The socialist paradise had not arrived, but perhaps the class war which preceded it had.

If the strikes and the depression had revealed anything, it was the need for change. Busts brought foreclosures and bankruptcy to the middle class. Workers wanted protection from exploitation, from the threat the unemployed posed to jobs and wages, and from the 'natural' servility they saw among 'non-European' labour. Farmers and rural labourers wanted protection against droughts and tumbling prices. In 'overgrown' and 'diseased' cities, comfortable people wanted protection from their poor neighbours' infections and supposed criminal habits. The poor wanted

The future had to be different.

a decent life, more secure workers wanted to keep the decency they had achieved. The future had to be different, not more of the same.

In the midst of depression and conflict, it is surprising that the separate colonies managed to federate into the Commonwealth of Australia by 1901 The relative economic power of one nation as opposed to six colonies convinced some. Those worried about defence saw a safer future in nation-building within the world's greatest empire. At the 1890 Australasian Federation conference, elder statesman Henry Parkes assured his audience that Australians had "made such progress as has excited the admiration of the best of other countries". Yet if he hoped for a pro-federation crusade, he would remain disappointed.

The idea of federation remained more popular outside the official political process, with the Australasian Natives' Association and the Federal Leagues reviving

A nation had apparently been made.

it again at conferences in Corowa in 1893 and Bathurst three years later. Elected conventions began discussing the details in 1897. Less populous states feared domination by New South Wales, while New South Wales doubted its need to dominate them. There was also the thorny question of which government—state or federal—would hold contentious powers like collecting taxes.

Nationalists disliked the remaining ties of dependence on Britain. Conservatives worried about the implications of a national government in which the vast majority of the citizens—even women and the poor— might exert their votes against society's natural leaders. The rapid rise of the Australian Labor Party, which captured its first seats in New South Wales in 1891 and briefly held power in Queensland in 1899, was also worrying. Inventing the political structures of a new nation was a risky business, especially as the decision to federate was to rest on colony-by-colony popular referenda.

The finer details were hammered out at the federal conventions of 1897 and 1898, and the voters of Victoria, Tasmania and South Australia quickly ratified the new Constitution. Having secured some amendments, New South Wales and Queensland joined in 1899. The British Parliament ratified the agreement in 1900, despite the dithering of Western Australia, which merged into the new Commonwealth one month after Britain had officially created it. On 1 January 1901, Commonwealth Inauguration Day, celebrations were held all over the new country. Processions, floats and banners, bad poetry and worse songs; a nation had apparently been made.

The political bonds of nationhood were now secure. Western Australians did vote to secede in the 1930s; the British government's refusal to consider their petition made civil war their only—unlikely—option. Other movements tried unsuccessfully to create new states in northern Queensland and southern New South Wales. The states grumbled about Commonwealth powers, but the Constitution ensured that extending those powers by referendum would be difficult. Indeed, a complex 'checks and balances' structure always served inertia far more successfully than initiative.

Imagining the shared destiny of Australians still caused disagreement. There were hard-headed economic concerns: labour leaders talked of nationalising and taxing; manufacturers of tariffs and profits; farmers of markets and trade. There was a jumble of patriotisms based on different versions of Australia's relationship with the old world. Adherence to empire or nationalism jostled with loyalties to religion, region and class. If journalists, politicians and artists are any guide, for every vision of a future splendid there was a warning about decline and decay.

Defining what the new nation owed its citizens, and citizens their nation, took some time. Concerns about Australia's small European population on the borders of a 'teeming' Asia focused attention on population growth and defence. Prolific motherhood was the Australian woman's duty. As the average Australian family shrank from six or seven children in the 1870s to just three by 1910, demands that women fulfil their national and racial responsibilities produced the first maternity allowances alongside royal commissions and campaigns against contraceptive devices and evils like prostitution and venereal disease.

If women were the mothers of Australia, men were its guardians and its soldiers. To defend British interests, Australians went to the Boer War. To safeguard Australia, the new national government instituted compulsory military training for boys and spent nearly a third of its income on defence by 1913.

Popular magazines and novels played out fantasies of war in blood-curdling tales of Japanese invasions, 'mongrel races' and opiated 'Chinamen' luring white women into sexual slavery. The shock of Japan's victory over Russia in 1905 only increased concerns about the 'white man's place' in Asia. Australian officials urged stronger Pacific defences, and made sure that the United States Great White Fleet included Australia on its world voyage in 1908. Australian visitors to imperial conferences asked for more consultation in strategic decisions, but they were never able to secure the empire they wanted.

With real imperial power securely in London, Australians could do little but hope that Anglo-Saxon loyalties would ensure their protection. Accordingly, defence meant not just military preparedness, but keeping Australia British enough to warrant that protection. There was fundamental consensus about the need to maintain racial purity, and the first real business of the new Federal Parliament was a unanimous commitment to 'white Australia'. There would be no immigration of 'alien coloured people', and there were proposals to remove those already in Australia. Aboriginals, of course, could not easily be deported. But segregated into government reserves, Australia's first inhabitants were a problem all too easily ignored .

The idea that Australia should safeguard its citizens was a central theme in the 'New Protection' promoted by liberal politicians such as Alfred Deakin and activist judges like H. B. Higgins. Its genius was to link tariffs to the protection of working men's wages. Proclaiming government's reponsibility to act for the collective good, it offered to balance the clashing interests of employers and workers, which had generated so much conflict in the 1890s. The New Protection captured and strengthened the spirit of reformist 'amelioration' in areas like education, town planning and public health. It also idealised Australian society as an antipodean 'social laboratory', and the Australian people as a progressive lesson to the old world.

The New Protection also told Australians how they were bound together. For children, there was free education and protection against moral evils. For mothers, there were allowances, and the celebration of their role in the "production of a physically, morally and intellectually well-developed citizenship". For every (white) adult, there was universal suffrage. For the elderly, there was the security of old-age pensions. And the whole structure relied upon and celebrated the breadwinning father, for whom compulsory arbitration and wage determination guaranteed an income sufficient to keep a family. Expecting all citizens to fulfil their 'natural' role, the protective nation promised security to people who remembered its absence all too well.

Amid the bargains and compromises, there were still disagreements. Attempts to impose political unity and allegiance to the empire did not overcome other loyalties. When the nation's children had to be forcefully taught just whose loyal children they were, when political coalitions formed and sundered with equal regularity, and when the Cardinal of Sydney celebrated Empire Day as 'Australia Day' and flew the flags of Ireland and Australia but not the United Kingdom, there could be little doubt that, at end of its first decade as a nation, Australia's future could still be imagined very differently.

Gallipoli came to stand for self-sacrifice.

III

IN 1914 Australia's political representatives agreed on their response to the outbreak of European war: Labor Prime Minister Andrew Fisher offered the "last man and last shilling". Billy Hughes, a long-time advocate of citizen defence, called the war "the gravest crisis of our history", confident that all Australians identified with a history and a home somewhat removed from their everyday experience.

Unemployment and rural depression helped swell the numbers of volunteers for the first Australian Imperial Force (AIF). War promised adventure for some; others fought for an empire they clearly felt beholden to. There was little doubt that Australia should help Britain, even if some fervent patriots were unwilling to consider sacrificing their lucrative contracts with German companies. Australia did its bit in 1914, quietly occupying Germany's Pacific territories. The *Sydney* sank the *Emden* in the Indian Ocean. The

20 000 men of the AIF landed in Egypt and, joining New Zealanders, formed the Australian and New Zealand Army Corps (ANZAC).

These soldiers, landed alongside British and French troops at Gallipoli to pressure Turkey and relieve hard-pressed Russia, would come to personify the war experience and even Australia itself. Seven thousand died of wounds and diseases in the eight months it took the British commanders to realise this was a lost cause. Yet death in vain only magnified their nobility, even among those who had actually seen war at close hand. Gallipoli came to stand for sacrifice and for that moment when Australia, through its young men, had proved itself. 'Gallipoli' and 'Anzac' gave Australia and its 'diggers' a place and a name at the centre of the world's history.

In time, 'Anzac' would become a story about 'warriors' and a 'race'—and their enemies—in which actual soldiers became less and less important. For the soldiers who had moved to France, many to later die in pointless charges at Pozières or Bullecourt, for the maimed and blinded, and for those who fought in Palestine, the Anzac story could explain the unexplainable. For those who lost their men, Anzac sacrifice and honour provided some answer to the question 'why?' Many needed answers: by the end of a war in which 330 000 Australians had served, one in six had been killed, half wounded, and even the physically unharmed would hear the guns of war for years to come.

The Anzac story implied national unity but by 1915 Australians were also identifying enemies among themselves. For Hughes, now Prime Minister, conscription for overseas service became the touchstone. His insistence on shared sacrifice might have sounded better if his government had not abandoned its attempt to control profits; with wages controlled by arbitration, it is hardly surprising that this conjured up images of bloated 'war profiteers'. And 'accepting the people's verdict' sounded hollow when anti-conscription meetings were broken up and Irish Catholics were indirectly or directly accused of lacking patriotism. For the referendum in late 1916, the pro-conscription campaign was vociferous and confident. When Australians narrowly voted against conscription, those who had argued for a 'yes' vote were stunned.

Conscriptionists were expelled from the Labor Party, but anti-conscriptionists were, at least figuratively, expelled from the nation. Huge strikes in 1917, notably in New South Wales, intensified charges of 'conspiracy' against the war effort. Dissenters were evil: Catholics became 'Sinn Fein' fanatics, unionists became 'radicals'—or, when the concept became available, 'Bolsheviks'—and feminists in the Women's Peace Army were labelled 'traitors'. Allowing the Australian people one more chance to get it right, Hughes organised a second referendum for December 1917. It lost by a larger margin than the first. Australia's war provided a national hero in the Anzac, but it also opened up deep gulfs of feeling that no victory celebration could bridge.

Impassioned divisions dominated the post-war period, and the Anzac legend crafted by official war historian C. E. W. Bean became the primary weapon against disloyalty. Bean's digger was an antidote, a sacrificing man who stood against division and dissent. This Anzac was no longer a real soldier; indeed, real returning soldiers were an unstable element in post-war society. Veterans' organisations quickly gained tremendous political clout, though as their links to conservative politics increased during the early 1920s, fewer real diggers remained members. But with Labor virtually destroyed by the conscription debate, and unions locked in a ferocious battle with employers to restore pre-war living standards, there was no force powerful enough to represent those diggers who spoke for something other than unthinking loyalty.

Post-war Australians recoiled from the revelation of internal dissent and from a world full of threats. Quarantining the nation made even more sense after influenza killed 12 000 people in 1919. Well into the 1930s, authorities sought to close the country against contagions: modern art and literature, 'unAustralian political ideas', 'Negro' music, even comics. Australians who ventured anywhere but Britain were in peril, not least the great horse Phar Lap and the great boxer Les Darcy, who both died mysterious deaths in America.

The great horse Phar Lap

And 'bodyline' cricket showed that even traditional friends could not always be trusted.

'Loyalty' became the defence against a fearful tomorrow. Nationalism no longer argued that Australia should change, or accommodate dissenting opinions. It was a grim celebration, a way of holding the line against anybody who questioned what all Australians were supposed to share. As one patriot argued in 1921, "it was damnable to think that any man should be allowed to be disloyal and live in a free country".

Movements for change did not simply fade away; feminists, in particular, remained active throughout the 1920s and 1930s, first in campaigns for child endowment and later on issues such as equal pay. Yet they were also affected by the need to avoid 'disloyalty'. Rumours of a communist march on Melbourne, which led to trench-digging in Victorian towns from Ouyen to Bairnsdale in 1931, were ludicrous, but the presence of respectable and powerful citizens in secret anti-Bolshevik armies suggests how weak their commitment to political freedom really was.

After 1920, with rural interests falling in behind the new Country Party, Nationalist Prime Minister

Stanley Bruce was increasingly identified with an ethos of aggressive national development, captured in the slogan 'Australia Unlimited' and the search for 'men, money and markets'. The 'men' (many were women) were Britons sent to the dominions through the Empire Settlement Scheme, and the money was British capital. The markets, too, were imperial, secured through a preference scheme for Australian wheat and wool.

American capital arrived, too, and with it came American ideas about 'industrial efficiency'. Much government policy reflected the confidence that scientific (and cost-saving) solutions could be found for all manner of human dilemmas. Substanial rhetoric—and smaller endowments—promoted 'rational' motherhood, while pre-marital examinations for hereditary defects were available in a small number of Racial Hygiene Clinics. Though Australia saw little sterilisation of the supposedly 'unfit', some proponents of eugenics spoke carelessly enough about 'useless' elements in the 'racial stock'.

For all the talk of Australia Unlimited, the 1920s were not particularly prosperous. Farmers and rural workers continued to struggle for a living. Empire Scheme and soldier settlers were rewarded with land at the very edge of agricultural viability, and suffered intensely from droughts and floods and everything else. Middle-class suburban homes had a radio, a gas stove, perhaps a refrigerator, but working families could afford few of these. One of the characteristics of 1920s prosperity was its dramatic unevenness. Bruce's government harried the unions into submission, confident that securing a 'good business climate' was more important than the socialist madness of redistributing wealth. In 1929, the government's electoral defeat signalled concern over falling living standards and rising industrial conflict. Yet as the new Labor government took office, more than one observer was warning of a possibly sharp dip in Australia's economic fortunes.

Because Australia depended so heavily on European and American prosperity, the world-wide economic

The Great Depression

depression of the 1930s hit with particular force. Constricted overseas loans put added pressure on export income at the very moment that prices for wheat and wool were plummeting. Governments cut spending, removing even more money from a deflating economy. Banks restricted loans, larger businesses cut wages and smaller businesses simply closed down, throwing thousands out of work. As incomes fell, so did people's spending power, further lowering prices and profits and bankrupting more businesses. Like an unhealthy engine, the nation's economy sputtered, wheezed and, for a time, seemed about to seize up entirely.

Early remedies compounded the problems, as nations like Australia tried to insulate themselves behind tariff walls. Tinkering with taxes, or charging for schools and health care, did little. By 1931, nearly a quarter of the working population was unemployed and tens of thousands of others were working for reduced wages.

Finding remedies meant finding someone who should carry the burden. The Bank of England sent Sir Otto Niemeyer to assess Australia's ability to service its debts. His solution was to restore 'sound financial management' by slashing wages and spending. The federal Treasurer, E. G. Theodore, favoured expansionary programmes to provide work for the unemployed. New South Wales Labor Premier Jack Lang, elected in 1930 with a mandate to resist cuts, proposed to simply stop paying interest on overseas loans.

The compromise Premiers' Plan of 1931 raised taxes, cut interest rates and enforced a 20 per cent cut in pensions. The wealthy would endure lower interest payments, pensioners and the unemployed would endure near-starvation. Governments developed public works schemes, and provided a suitably undignified 'sustenance' dole of rations. Company profits, which had fallen steeply at first, virtually recovered by 1932, just as unemployment reached its peak of 30 per cent. Voters did not thank Labor for this 'equality' of sacrifice.

The generation scarred by the Depression would dominate Australian life well into the 1960s. A few welcomed its purging qualities, including some managing directors who welcomed the fall of troublesome competitors. Some said it proved the inadequacy of representative government, and admired the rigorous efficiencies of European fascism. The Labor Party was savaged by defections and infighting, while conservative groups like the All for Australia Leagues joined the new United Australia Party. There were a few riots and calls for revolution, and the Communist Party of Australia increased its membership, but the 'threat' from the left was always less significant in real life than in the minds of the nervous.

Silent suffering reflected the demoralising effect of unemployment and the swift action of police against any collective response to eviction or the daily indignities of welfare. The Depression picked off the vulnerable, and brought real want back into homes that had only recently escaped it. Teachers and public servants scraped by on reduced salaries, salesmen lived on the week's commission. While welfare officials discovered real malnutrition among inner-city children, charities struggled to sift out the 'deserving'. The poor helped each other as best they could. Many people would remember the added zest of pleasures— meat, jam instead of dripping, a movie—once taken for granted.

If the 1930s showed Australians nothing else, they showed what could happen to people in a society that didn't care. As yet, some refused to see, or offered only condescension: perhaps the poor simply needed to learn personal efficiency, perhaps babies should be removed from parents who taught them the habits of poverty. But others were shocked into seeing that people were impoverished by structures, not personal habits. Real change seemed impossible in the midst of economic crisis, but many Australians began to believe that the terrible insecurities of the 1930s should never be allowed to happen again.

Plans to change Australia's future direction stood a better chance once the nation was again at war in September 1939. After assurances that Britain would not forget the potential threat from Japan, a second AIF went to fight in North Africa and Greece during 1940 and 1941. But Australia's resources, diminished by ten years of depression, remained unmobilised. Fearful, perhaps, of sparking the same disagreements as in 1916, political leaders showed no great enthusiasm for 'total war'.

But total war came to Australia, and rapidly. Just weeks after Labor's John Curtin had formed a new government, the Japanese attacked the American fleet at Pearl Harbor. By Christmas 1941 they had occupied Hong Kong and most of Malaya and sunk the two most important ships in the British Navy. In mid-February, Singapore fell; within days, bombs had fallen on Darwin and the Japanese Army was landing in New Guinea. The old certainties were gone: white supremacy hadn't stopped the Japanese, the British Navy had proved ineffective, and Singapore's fall indicated that the empire's hold over Asia was broken forever. Curtin, demanding total mobilisation, declared that Australia would henceforth seek protection from the United States.

Roosevelt and Churchill's 'beat Hitler first' strategy frayed Australian nerves, but the arrival of General Douglas Macarthur and the first American troops confirmed Australia's importance as a base for operations

The hard-fought defence of New Guinea

against Japan. The Battle of the Coral Sea and the hard-fought defence of New Guinea seemed to lessen the immediate peril. Unwilling to press the contentious issue of conscription, Curtin simply extended the definition of 'home territory' in which conscripts could fight to include New Guinea, Indonesia and the South-west Pacific. By 1945 over half a million Australian men had served in the armed forces; hundreds of thousands of men and women had 'joined up' in other ways. Over 30 000 died: a third in Europe and North Africa, a third fighting the Japanese, a third of disease, starvation and brutality in Japanese prisoner-of-war camps.

Less costly in lives than World War I, this war had a far greater impact on everyday life. Resources and people were more effectively mobilised. Civilians were directed into essential war work or agricultural production. For many, especially women, this meant unexpected physical mobility, access to paid work, and opportunities to learn skills, along with a profound mixing together of people from different places. Their experience of war was also spiced by the arrival of American soldiers whose Hollywood looks, Coca-Cola and chewing gum attracted some and infuriated others. World War II opened and stirred up Australian society as no other event had.

For Aboriginal people, wartime service raised hopes that post-war society might, for the first time, include them in the nation they had helped to save. At the 1943 Women's Charter Conference, feminists outlined their hopes for post-war society. Both were part of a broader expectation that after the war, strong, activist governments should plan and create the good society. Such hopes stemmed in large part from the unprecedented power the federal government was now able to command. It had proved itself capable of mobilising and defending a nation under fire. It had rationed, conscripted and controlled, and reformers saw no reason why planning to "cover the whole life of the citizen" should end with the war. Indeed, there was no reason why the world as a whole should not become a more predictable, peaceful place, and Australia played a significant role in the attempt to create a workable United Nations.

The extension of federal powers, notably over the collection of income tax and the provision of social welfare, was hotly contested by the states, stymied at a 1944 referendum, and always threatened by conservative High Court interpretations of the constitution. What was achievable under defence powers would be lost in the peace. Yet in its Department of Post-war Reconstruction, and the white papers and planning agencies it sponsored, the Labor government produced a blueprint for change, and an argument that governments owed obligations—including the preservation of full employment—to citizens. During the last years of the war, governments came as close as they ever would to ensuring that a market economy would also be expected to deliver a better and more equal society.

The closeness of the Japanese advance evoked old fears of an 'empty continent' and traditional remedies: encouraging reproduction, developing the nation's north, and filling the empty spaces with hard-working migrants. By the war's close, Australians were getting married in unprecedented numbers, and had already begun creating the 'baby boom'. Grand schemes, such as the audacious dams and tunnels in the Snowy Mountains, demanded workers, and that meant migrants. Many British people did come, but the new Minister for Immigration, Arthur Calwell, soon had to cast his net wider: 'displaced persons' from Eastern Europe, Germans, Dutch, Italians, Greeks, Maltese, Yugoslavs, Lebanese, Turks. A social and cultural revolution began, though if they read the official prescriptions about not 'standing out', people from Calabria and Macedonia would not have predicted that.

Others feared that wartime prosperity would give way to renewed depression. Reformers could not easily dispel those anxieties. Accepting austerity in hope of better things to come was a lot to ask people frustrated by continued rationing of petrol, tea and butter or sharing cramped flats because there were no bricks to build houses. Unions, wary of an economy which had never before boomed without busting soon after, pushed for better wages. In many industries, employers and workers seemed locked in confrontation. Bitter battles increased some workers' faith in the hard tactics of communist union leaders. Within unions, anti-communist 'industrial groups' harried the radicals, while the Catholic Church strove to convince its working-class parishioners that communism was evil. The Labor Party confronted 'hard-liners', most notably in the New South Wales coal strike of 1949, but was still abused in parliament and the press as 'socialistic'.

Reformers had certainly not predicted the resurgence of an astute new conservative force, with Robert Menzies, politically moribund in 1941, a surprising spearhead. The new Liberal Party happily kicked the communist can; they benefited even more from the financial resources of banks and doctors appalled by 'nationalisation' and from employers anxious for a government that better understood their needs.

Menzies was able to channel post-war anxieties into a search for security based not on social and economic reform, but on being left alone. He celebrated the self-sacrificing virtues of his 'forgotten people' against the selfish desires of the unworthy. In his most ingenious political strategy, Menzies also spoke directly to women, carefully evoking a female domestic realm threatened by shortages and strikes.

Menzies, voted into power in 1949

Conservatism identified some compelling villains. In Australia, Labor tends to promise long-term gains and a fairer society, while conservatism stresses sacrifice, security and standing firm against mostly imagined enemies. Voting Menzies into power at the 1949 election, some Australians clearly thought those enemies were real. Others, still carrying memories of depression and conflict, were understandably convinced that security now was more important than equality later.

The 1950s may look like a twilight broken only when 'social change' started again in the 1960s, but they were more than a quiet prelude to what came after. A suburban idyll, of men and motor mowers, and women busy tidying a world they played a significant part in making, grew out of uncertainty as much as hope. This was a careful tomorrow, because people prized safety in a world they knew could quickly turn dangerous.

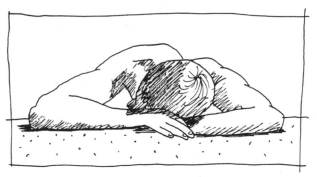

The Australian way of life

Unity was celebrated, but there were deep divides of politics and belief, which kept Australians apart. Catholics and Protestants lived and worked in almost separate worlds. Liberal voters despised unions and communist trouble-makers, Labor voters hated Menzies and the anti-communist 'groupers' who were destroying the party.

Wages and spending kept increasing. More people could afford refrigerators, washing machines, even cars. Menzies rewarded the middle class with tax concessions and benefits, and more public money for private health care and private schools. But one in seven Australians still lived in poverty, and sharp recessions showed the limits of affluence. A wage and welfare system which staked everything on protecting the bread-winner's livelihood offered little to people who were unable to work. Australia's healthy, happy children were paraded before the visiting Queen, but a panic about 'delinquent' youth showed the hard edges of an intolerant society. People carried in their minds the spectre of 'the bomb' and the fear of another war. If this was a time of prosperity and harmony, it was a very peculiar one.

The 1956 Melbourne Olympics

Conservatives seemed convinced that Australians should agree on everything. Attacking communists was handy in elections, though voters narrowly defeated an attempt to ban the Communist Party in 1951. Loyalists and anti-communists finally split the Labor Party in 1955. Still, even with the new Democratic Labor Party's preferences flowing to the Liberals, Menzies defeated the Australian Labor Party by just one seat in 1961. Consensus was never far from division.

Menzies personified Anglo-Australian superiority, even as the United States replaced Britain at the centre of international relationships. Australia supported Britain's attempts to remain a great power. When it needed to test its atomic weapons, Menzies offered uninhabited central Australia. Aboriginal people, apparently, still did not inhabit the land.

During the 1950s, the 'Australian way of life' replaced discredited ways of defining the nation, like 'race' and 'stock'. 'Way of life' was safer, vague enough to admit all kinds of prejudices. In a country accommodating so many 'New Australians', it was easier to insist that migrants abandon their culture than their 'breeding'. And taking Aboriginal children away from their parents was apparently beneficial when you only had to change their habits, not their race.

Confidence in a 'way of life' was never complete. Cultured critics lampooned suburban manners, deplored the 'Australian ugliness', or escaped the 'cultural cringe' by heading for England. Even the displays of Australian achievement had an uncertain edge. In two great events where the world was watching—the 1954 Royal Tour and the 1956 Melbourne Olympics—Australians worried they might somehow get it wrong. Fears of expanding communism in Asia tied the Australian government ever more securely to the United States, to the point of encouraging its troops into the jungles of Vietnam. Americans in South-east Asia were a reassuring signal that Australia would be safe.

By the mid-1960s, though, Australia had changed. When the Queen visited again in 1963, Menzies' adoration started to seem embarrassing. In any event, the Britain she represented was drowned out one year later by the different accents of the touring Beatles. Migrant Australians were working and raising their children alongside working-class Anglo-Australians.

Some people complained of 'dagos' taking jobs, but migrants' success rested on their willingness to ignore prejudice and help each other in institutions which blended regional differences into stronger 'Greek' or 'Italian' communities, and on the unheralded tolerance of their neighbours.

In other parts of rapidly growing cities, the children of the baby boom were nearing adulthood. Compared with every generation before them, they were better fed and less affected by penny-pinching and frustrated expectations. They had jobs, or could expect to get them easily. Some married, had their own children early and moved out to raw new suburbs. Others went off to university or teachers' college to gain the security their parents so desperately desired them to have. But a good number began to regard the world that had been made for them as a world they didn't really want.

Protests against conscription and Australia's involvement in the Vietnam War symbolise a shift that set one generation against another, spawned various social movements, and brought Labor back to power under Gough Whitlam in 1972. Yet the peace movement depended on veteran pacifists as well as students. And a resurgent feminism concerned with equal pay and equal opportunity reflected a movement of married women into the workforce begun by the mothers of 1970s women's liberationists.

The generations were separated by profoundly different expectations of the future, not the courage of conviction. For people raised in depression and war, the safe, secure world of the 1950s was an important emotional and psychological achievement. But their children often experienced that achievement as an imposed conformity. Reactions to different experiences were hard to combine. Daughters didn't want to be their mothers, and the contraceptive pill, legalised abortion, equal opportunity and easier divorce would be their guarantees. Sons thought they shared little with distant fathers, though men would take much longer than women to explore the meaning of that discovery. If there was a 'revolution', it began in homes and families, not on the street.

Instead of accepting authority as the price of safety, young people insisted on their right to speak and most of all to say no. Being different expressed pride and identity, not abnormality. People listened more carefully to previously marginalised activists who, in turn, assumed the forms and language of international political protest: indigenous rights, feminism, migrant identity, environmentalism, gay rights.

Reformist governments in Canberra and some states expressed and sometimes acted to endorse these demands. Aboriginal people, finally recognised as citizens in a 1967 referendum, revived the crucial question of land rights. Women's equality became political business. The White Australia policy and assimilation were abandoned in favour of a new term, 'multiculturalism'. With change came the resurgent nationalism of Australian art, Australian theatre and Australian culture.

Yet Whitlam's short-lived Labor government did not rely simply on social movements. In many parts of ordinary Australia, he is remembered for the first accessible health care, benefits for single parents and the elderly, better schools, and footpaths and sewers.

The dismissal of the Whitlam government

By 1975 the long economic boom which had begun in the 1950s was ending. Labor attempted to contain the problems, but Australia was always a victim of more powerful nations' economic troubles, however careful its own policies.

Understandings of the Whitlam government are dominated by its divisive conclusion. For some, Labor was not made for sound management. When the Governor-General dismissed the government in November 1975 they were relieved. Others felt that the whole momentum of change had been betrayed by an anachronism. In any event, questions about the dismissal were muffled by the sweeping conservative victory at the subsequent election.

If the new Liberal government of Malcolm Fraser differed little from Labor on foreign policy, migration and multiculturalism, traditional conservative targets again came under fire. Economic policy ensured that the unemployed and the low-paid would bear the worst cost of containing inflation. 'Unnecessary' government spending always seemed to mean money spent on the poor. And in blaming 'socialist' unions for their 'greed', Fraser's rhetoric hadn't moved that far from the red-baiting conservatism of the 1920s.

In eight years of growing economic and social problems, there were numerous reports but little action. Short-lived booms creating wealth for mineral companies and a few lucky workers did not bring back the prosperity of the 1960s, and the growing wealth of Queensland and Western Australia went hand in hand with the sinking fortunes of industrial areas in the southern states. 'Structural adjustment' was a clumsy euphemism for harder realities like structural unemployment and growing disparities of wealth between classes, regions and generations.

The sharp recession of 1982–83 helped to destroy the Fraser government's credibility and majority. Yet the 1970s experience had also changed Labor. Wary of antagonising those who had helped undo Whitlam, the new government would talk up change, but only by talking down the party's tradition of changing the distribution of economic rewards and penalties.

By the end of the 1980s it seemed that the centenary of federation might bring dramatic changes in the symbols and even the structures of the nation. Imagining Australia's future now involved celebrating its diversity, identifying Asian nations as trading partners rather than threats, recognising the legacies of Aboriginal dispossession and the fiction of *terra nullius*, and wondering whether Australia could outgrow its antagonistic relationship with its own geography and history.

Cultural diversity was finally celebrated, but differences based on wealth and class were still largely ignored. Labor's decision to 'open up' the flagging Australian economy to global forces may have been unavoidable, but decisions about who would carry the burden were never pre-ordained. Economic restructuring created some winners, but a larger number of losers. For those who kept their jobs, the Accord Labor struck with the trade unions held down wages, while corporate high-fliers rewarded themselves with fat bonuses and speculative investors won and lost millions. Basic infrastructure in health, transport and education began to fray, as governments privatised what they could and 'downsized' the rest.

After another grinding recession, commentators belatedly discovered entrenched unemployment and real misery during the 1990s. Successive Labor Prime Ministers Bob Hawke and Paul Keating reinvented Australia's future—as a 'clever country' or a 'working nation'—but they did not remake it. The major political parties have almost succeeded in convincing each other—and a good many voters—that Australia's future comes down to looking after yourself in a more and more privatised world. Government is now dominated by those who know how to cost but not to value, and the conservative election victory in 1996 may leave some Australians wondering whether a future made by and for the comfortable is a future that can include them.

Over its European history, doubt and confidence in Australia's future has persisted alongside debates about what kind of old world or new world this should be.

In popular environmentalism and tourism, more Australians are experiencing the age and the tenor of a different kind of land. Australia is still being discovered, slowly.

People in the future may judge that the 1990s marked a watershed in attitudes to wealth and inequality no less significant than the 1890s. They may remember environmental victories and the difficult arguments about development, rural livelihoods and conservation. They may celebrate the political will which started to take guns out of Australian homes yet ponder why it could not be repeated to create jobs and chances for the young. Perhaps their most significant questions though, will concern reconciliation and justice for Australia's original occupiers, once the High Court's endorsement of native title rights in the 1990 Mabo case finally established that Australians had to face the moral and legal consequences of their history.

For them, too, the past will be made up of moments when the future might have been different. And there are places in our past and our present where the truth is told about a history that encompasses tens of thousands of years, not a couple of hundred. The truth is not about guilt, but about responsibility and recognition. In the final years of the twentieth century, we still seem far from achieving that. There are discoveries—and rediscoveries—yet to be made.

Further Reading

The following works all provide a much more extended treatment of themes and issues discussed in this book, and are recommended as accessible and interesting explorations of Australian history.

Judith Brett, *Robert Menzies' Forgotten People*, Macmillan, Sydney 1992.

Richard Broome, *Aboriginal Australians: Black Responses to White Dominance*, 1788–1994, 2nd edn, Allen & Unwin, Sydney 1994.

Graeme Davison, *The Unforgiving Minute: How Australians Learned to Tell the Time*, Oxford University Press, Melbourne 1993.

Tim Flannery, *The Future Eaters: An Ecological History of the Australian Lands and People*, Reed Books, Sydney 1994.

David Goodman, *Gold Seeking: Victoria and California in the 1850s*, Allen & Unwin, Sydney 1994.

Tom Griffiths, *Hunters and Collectors: The Antiquarian Imagination in Australia*, Cambridge University Press, Melbourne 1996.

Patricia Grimshaw, Marilyn Lake, Ann McGrath and Marian Quartly, *Creating a Nation, 1788–1990*, McPhee Gribble, Melbourne 1994.

Janet McCalman, *Struggletown: Public and Private Life in Richmond, 1900–1965*, Melbourne University Press, Melbourne 1984.

Janet McCalman, *Journeyings: The Biography of a Middle-Class Generation 1920–1990*, Melbourne University Press, Melbourne 1993.

Stuart Macintyre, *The Oxford History of Australia, Volume 4: The Succeeding Age, 1901–1942*, Oxford University Press, Melbourne 1986.

Andrew Markus, *Australian Race Relations, 1788–1993*, Allen & Unwin, Sydney 1994.

Henry Reynolds, *The Other Side of the Frontier: Aboriginal Resistance to the European Invasion of Australia*, Penguin, Melbourne 1982.

John Rickard, *Australia: A Cultural History*, 2nd edn, Longman, London 1997.

Alistair Thomson, *Anzac Memories: Living with the Legend*, Oxford University Press, Melbourne 1994.

Richard White, *Inventing Australia: Images and Identity, 1688–1980*, Allen & Unwin, Sydney 1981.

Darwin

NO[RTHERN]
TE[RRITORY]

WESTERN
AUSTRALIA

• Kalgoorlie

Perth